The Final Trial of Richard III

A One-Act

Courtroom Drama

by

MARY W. SCHALLER

THE DRAMATIC PUBLISHING COMPANY

THE FINAL TRIAL OF RICHARD III

A One-Act Courtroom Drama
for Sixteen Men, Eight Women, with doubling∗

CAST LIST

BAILIFF
TIME .... the judge
HISTORY .... the prosecutor
RUMOR .... assistant prosecutor
RICHARD III .... the defendant
CHARITY .... defense counsel
SIR THOMAS MORE .... historian
WILLIAM SHAKESPEARE .... playwright
COUNTESS OF DESMOND ...... a child in the court of
     Edward IV & an old lady in the court of Elizabeth I
QUEEN ELIZABETH WOODVILLE .. wife of Edward IV
QUEEN ANNE NEVILLE .... wife of Richard III
CLERK OF THE COURT

THE LORD CHAMBERLAIN'S MEN:
PLAYERS-WITHIN-THE-PLAY

PLAYER RICHARD .... the Player
BRACKENBURY .... lieutenant of the Tower
GEORGE, DUKE OF CLARENCE ... brother of Edward
                         IV & Richard III
PRINCE EDWARD .... Little Prince in the Tower
RICHARD, DUKE OF YORK . Little Prince in the Tower
DUKE OF BUCKINGHAM .... supporter of Richard III
                   who turned traitor
JAMES TYRREL .... henchman of Richard III
DIGHTON .... murderer one
FORREST .... murderer two
CATESBY .... supporter of Richard III
HENRY TUDOR .... later King Henry VII
ANNE NEVILLE, the Player .... Edward IV's Queen
GHOST OF EDWARD OF LANCASTER .... Anne's first
                   husband

GHOST OF HENRY VI .... father of Edward of
Lancaster

MESSENGER

*NOTE: The PLAYERS, with the exceptions of RICH-
ARD, ANNE, ELIZABETH, GEORGE, and THE LIT-
TLE PRINCES can take double parts.

TIME: The Eve of the 500th Anniversary of the Battle of
Bosworth Field

PLACE: A Courtroom in Eternity

THE FINAL TRIAL OF RICHARD III was first performed on November 16, 1985 at Washington Irving
School, Springfield, Virginia by the Shakespeare Class of
the Fairfax County Recreation Department.

ORIGINAL CAST

Richard III, the defendant .... Jerry Reece
Time .... Kurt Bose
Bailiff .... Keene Parker
Clerk .... Terri Anderson
History .... Kala Leggett
Rumor .... Kathleen Robinson
Charity .... Libby Goodwin
Sir Thomas More .... Meaghan Parker
William Shakespeare .... Shannon Sheehan
Queen Elizabeth, wife of Edward IV .... Julie Harman
Queen Anne, wife of Richard III .... Stephanie Penny
Countess of Desmond .... Julie Zielaskiewicz

ORIGINAL CAST

THE LORD CHAMBERLAIN'S MEN

Richard III, the Player .... Pat Sheehan
Murderer One .... Lance Murchison
Murderer Two .... Patrika Mani
Murderer Three .... Sabrina Sandusky
Brackenbury .... Bridget Casucci
Duke of Clarence .... Bill Wright
Prince Edward .... Cami St. Germain
Duke of York .... Carol Blosser
Duke of Buckingham .... Anne Turner
Queen Elizabeth, the Player .... Donnis McMullin
Queen Anne, the Player .... Suzen Mason
Tyrrel .... Kathleen Burns
Dighton .... Kim Christie-Mill
Ghost of Edward of Lancaster .... Michelle Saari
Ghost of Henry VI .... Mark Lane
Henry Tudor .... Brian Cabe

Assistant Director .... Brian Cabe
Stage Managers .... Mark Lane and Michelle Saari

To the original cast and crew,
for whom it was written,
and most especially,
to Jerry,
with my deep appreciation.

M.W.S.

THE FINAL TRIAL OF RICHARD III

PROLOGUE: *The curtain is closed. The BAILIFF steps before the curtain and speaks directly to the audience.*

BAILIFF. Welcome to the final trial of Richard III. Richard III was a complex man: a scholar who was forced to become a soldier; a relentless general who built churches and founded colleges. He learned the art of warfare and executions without trial from the most ruthless man of the age, the Earl of Warwick, known to history as "The Kingmaker." Richard learned to kill before he was old enough to learn to love. He was born at the height of the gangster brawls known afterward as the Wars of the Roses: York against Lancaster. The prize was the crown of England itself. The times were violent and Richard was thrust into the forefront of events by Destiny. Richard was born in the Middle Ages. At his death on Bosworth Field thirty-two years later, the Renaissance had already dawned. He was a man caught in the transition of the times. Was he as evil and as cold-blooded as his reputation would have us believe? Or was Richard III a reflection of his period? By the magic of Theatre, you, our audience, will cease to be mere spectators of what is to follow. Instead, you have stepped into the framework of our drama and have now become the jury at our trial. You, ladies and gentlemen of the jury, will listen to the testimony. You will weigh the evidence. You will render the verdict. Ladies and gentlemen of the jury, "your humble patience we pray: gently to hear and kindly to judge our play."

SCENE: *The curtain opens to reveal a Courtroom in Eternity. The BAILIFF walks into the scene and takes his place at the rear of the Gallery section. The JUDGE's bench, which is currently vacant, and the witness box*

7

*are downstage right. At the UC stage position is the
prosecution table where HISTORY and RUMOR are going
over their notes. The defense table is downstage of
them. RICHARD III is seated alone at this table. His
wife, ANNE NEVILLE, is seated just behind him in the
first row of the Gallery. The Gallery is filled with the
remaining members of the cast, including the players.*

BAILIFF. Hear ye, hear ye, this court is now in session.
Draw near and give attention all who have business in
this court. The Right Honorable Judge, Venerable
Time, presiding. All rise.

*(All stand as TIME, in judge's robes and wig enters and
seats himself at the bench.)*

BAILIFF. Be seated. *(All sit.)*
TIME. Master Bailiff, please read the indictment.
BAILIFF. Your Honor, ladies and gentlemen of the
jury, the indictment reads as follows: that Richard,
Duke of Gloucester and afterward King of England,
known as Richard III, being ill-formed both of body
and of mind, did willfully murder or caused to be
murdered the following persons: Henry VI; Edward,
Prince of Lancaster; George, Duke of Clarence; Edward
V; his brother, Richard, Duke of York and Queen
Anne, his own wife, thus branding Richard III as the
most evil king in English history. *(RICHARD visibly
controls his anger at these charges.)* This court has
been convened to settle once and for all these
accusations.
TIME. Thank you, Master Bailiff. The indictment
against Richard III has been read. Is the prosecution
present?
HISTORY *(rising)*. We are, Your Honor.
TIME. Master History, is it? So *you* are the Prosecutor?
HISTORY. So please the court, Your Honor. I am well-
acquainted with this case, having pursued it for the
last 500 years.
TIME. I see. Very well, then. I note that you have an

assistant counselor. Introduce her to the court for the record.

HISTORY. Your Honor, the Lady Rumor is my associate. She, too, is well-versed in this matter.

RUMOR (*standing*). So please Your Honor.

TIME. It does not please me much to see History and Rumor together in this case.

HISTORY. We have often worked together before, Your Honor.

TIME. I am well aware of that, Master History, and many times it has been an ill-matched union. Nevertheless, since Rumor had a great hand in this matter in the past, I will allow her to remain, however she is *your* responsibility.

HISTORY. Yes, Your Honor. (*HISTORY and RUMOR sit down.*)

TIME. Is the defense here present?

RICHARD. I am, Your Honor. (*Rises.*)

TIME. Richard III! Where is your defense counselor?

RICHARD. Your Honor, my name and reputation have been so blackened over the centuries that no lawyer will take my case. But it is no matter. I will represent myself, as I always have, in my own defense.

TIME. To be fair, you must have some legal counsel in these proceedings. Is there no one here who would undertake to represent the defendant, Richard III? (*Silence.*) No one at all?

CHARITY (*rising from her place in the back of the Gallery*). Your Honor, though I am not prepared for this case, I cannot stand by and see this man be defenseless and alone against the world. I'll defend him to the best of my ability, so please the court.

TIME. Approach the bench and be recognized.

CHARITY (*coming forward*). I am Charity, Your Honor. I am seldom seen in court.

RUMOR (*snickering*). Charity! Then our case is as good as won right now if Richard's only defense is Charity!

TIME. Silence! Silence in this court!

HISTORY (*rising*). We welcome Mistress Charity to the bar, Your Honor.

TIME. And so you should. Richard III, do you accept Charity as your court-appointed defense counsel?

RICHARD. Your Honor, I wish to remain as my own counselor as I know more of the facts at hand. If you and Charity will agree, she can be my assistant in legal matters.

TIME. Charity?

CHARITY. I accept, Your Honor.

TIME. Very well, I will allow it. Take your place and proceed.

RUMOR (*as CHARITY seats herself next to RICHARD*). Charity! Is that all he can come up with?

HISTORY (*aside*). Quiet! Do you want to get us thrown out of court? Time can be a stern judge.

RUMOR. It's of no matter to me. The case is won already.

TIME. The prosecution, if they are ready, may present their opening statement to the jury.

HISTORY (*rising and coming center*). We are, Your Honor.

TIME. Proceed.

HISTORY (*addressing the audience*). Ladies and gentlemen of the jury, we have come together this day to see that justice, true justice, may be served once and for all. We intend to prove beyond a shadow of a doubt that Richard III richly deserves the names of Murderer Villain and Devil Incarnate and that he should be forevermore considered unworthy of any place in Eternity save the blackest hole of Hell. In his lifetime, this man, this so-called king, cut a swathe of blood through the length and breadth of England, killing two kings, a brother, nephews, friends and even his own wife to achieve his evil ends. He loved no one, trusted no one and was loyal to none but himself. He deserves eternal condemnation and damnation. (*He returns to his seat as the gallery reacts.*)

TIME. Has the defense an opening statement?

CHARITY (*rises and comes to the center*). Your Honor, ladies and gentlemen of the jury, in the interest of justice and future generations, my client, Richard III, wishes to clear his name of the slanders and the lies under which, for five centuries now, he has lived. We ask the court to take into consideration that, thanks to the many writers employed by the Tudor rulers, the good name of Richard III has been given "bad press" - blotted and smeared with the mud thrown by hate and fear. The defense feels that the jury may be prejudiced against the defendant before this trial even starts and we request that the jury keep an open mind to what we shall present for their consideration. Ladies and gentlemen, do not judge yet but, in the true spirit of justice for all upon which our laws are based, open your minds and hearts and let *them* be your guides. (*CHARITY returns to her seat.*)

TIME. Thank you, Counselor. The jury is so instructed. Is the prosecution ready to call its first witness?

HISTORY (*rising*). We are, Your Honor. We call Sir Thomas More to the stand.

BAILIFF. Sir Thomas More come into court! (*MORE rises from the Gallery and is escorted by the BAILIFF to the witness box.*) Do you swear to tell the truth, the whole truth and nothing but the truth, so help you God?

MORE. I do.

BAILIFF. Be seated and state your name and occupation for the record. (*MORE sits as BAILIFF returns to his place.*)

MORE. Sir Thomas More, scholar and writer. I was Lord Chancellor under Henry VIII.

HISTORY (*coming center*). You are considered to be one of the most brilliant men of your age, are you not?

MORE. You are kind to say so, sir.

HISTORY. And among your writings you authored the book, *Utopia* a perennial best seller?

MORE. College professors seem to enjoy it.

HISTORY. And you were canonized a Saint of the Catholic Church after your death?

MORE. It is an honor I neither looked for nor feel worthy of.

HISTORY. Therefore we may assume that whatever you

write would surely have a great deal of thought and truth behind it?

MORE. Yes, as much as it is possible to do so.

HISTORY (*taking some papers from his table*). Your Honor, I have here excerpts from a book by Sir Thomas More entitled *History of Richard III* which I would like to introduce at this time.

TIME. Does the defense have any objection?

CHARITY. No, Your Honor.

TIME. Very well. Clerk, mark the pages as Exhibit A. (*CLERK does so.*) Proceed, Counselor.

HISTORY (*handing the pages to MORE*). Sir Thomas, do you recognize these pages?

MORE. I do.

HISTORY. And did you, in fact, write them?

MORE. I did.

HISTORY. Would you please read aloud to the court the passages I have marked?

MORE (*reading*). "Richard III was little of stature, ill featured of limb, crook back, his left shoulder much higher than his right; hard-favored visage. He was malicious, wrathful, envious..."

RICHARD (*jumping to his feet*). Objection!

CHARITY (*also rising*). Your Honor, we would like to register an objection to this slanderous testimony but we will allow the prosecution to continue...

RICHARD (*looking at CHARITY unbelievingly*). Continue!?!

CHARITY. ...to continue his line of questioning. We will refute this statement at a later time. (*CHARITY and RICHARD sit, RICHARD very much disturbed.*)

TIME. I will take note of your objection. Proceed, Master History.

HISTORY. Sir Thomas, why would you write such a description?

MORE. My intention was to show that Richard III's evil character was reflected in his physical appearance.

CHARITY (*rising*). Objection! It has not been proven that Richard possesses an evil character.

TIME. Sustained.

HISTORY. I have no further questions. (*Returns to his seat*.)

TIME (*to CHARITY*). You may cross-examine the witness.

RICHARD (*rising*). If it so please the court, I would like to question this man myself.

TIME. That is your right.

RICHARD. Thank you, Your Honor.

CHARITY (*aside to RICHARD*). Tread softly, my lord. He is a formidable witness.

RICHARD (*comes to center stage*). Sir Thomas More, when did you write this so-called *History*.

MORE. I wrote the first draft in 1513 but it wasn't published until 1543.

RICHARD. In 1543? You mean it was published after your death?

MORE. Yes.

RICHARD. And was this "history" of yours in a finished state when it was finally published?

MORE. No, it was not. It was garbled and incomplete. I got caught up in other matters and never had the time to polish the manuscript.

RICHARD. Obviously. In your first sentence you write that my brother, the late Edward IV, died at the age of 50. Are you aware that this is incorrect? My brother was 40 when he died.

MORE. As I told you, the manuscript was in rough draft.

RICHARD. To write such a description of me, you must have seen me.

MORE. No, I was barely seven when you died.

RICHARD. Then where did you get such a vile description of me?

MORE. From my tutor, Bishop Morton.

RICHARD. Ah, my old friend, Bishop Morton. 'Tis true. He did know me. Did he like me?

MORE. No. You had him imprisoned by the Duke of Buckingham for supporting the Woodville family and the Lancasterians against you.

RICHARD. As a king, was I not within my rights to

imprison any powerful man who openly spoke treason against me?

MORE. That is the law.

RICHARD. And so, instead of executing Bishop Morton for treason as you seem to have me doing to everyone else, I merely imprison him. In gratitude for his life, he escaped to France where he joined forces with Henry Tudor against me. And tell me, Sir Thomas, what became of Bishop Morton under my successor?

MORE. Henry VII created him the Archbishop of Canterbury.

RICHARD. Which is the highest churchman in the land. And he, being your tutor, you naturally presumed he spoke the truth about me.

MORE. Naturally, he was a good man.

RICHARD. Who, as it happened, hated me. Tell me this, historian, did *you* write the truth?

MORE. As I perceived it then.

RICHARD. And if, in your research, you had found that Henry Tudor had unlawfully usurped my throne and that he and his family ruled without legal right, would you have written *that* down?

MORE. If that were the case, I don't believe I would have written *anything* down.

RICHARD. How so?

MORE. For such writings as that would be treason.

RICHARD. Therefore, if you paint Richard III as an evil monster, the government honors you but if you write the truth, heads will roll. Yours did.

MORE. That was another matter entirely.

RICHARD. You called *me* a monster when you served one yourself?

MORE. Henry VIII was a complex man.

RICHARD. Complex! He had six wives; beheaded two of them; broke with Rome; pillaged the monasteries; and not only executed every friend he ever had, not to mention a whole abbeyful of Carthusian monks, but he even managed to martyr a saint of the Church - you!

HISTORY (*rising*). Objection!

RICHARD. Not even *I* could do all that! And yet, I'm the blackest king who ever ruled!?!

HISTORY. Objection, Your Honor! Henry VIII is not on trial here!

TIME. Sustained. Counselor, please instruct your client to stick to the point.

CHARITY *(aside to RICHARD)*. Take care, my lord. Questioning a saint is dangerous business.

RICHARD. Sir Thomas, as Chancellor of England and as a scholar and historian, could you please tell the court what sort of a king England needed during the time known as the Wars of the Roses?

MORE *(to the audience)*. The country needed a strong king. The crown of England belonged to anyone who could seize it and hold on to it. Your brother, Edward IV, came to the throne by deposing Henry VI, who was a weak king, if I may say so. In earlier times, Richard II died on the orders of Henry Bolingbroke who then became Henry IV. Henry Tudor defeated you in battle and became Henry VII. The Wars of The Roses were very violent times.

RICHARD. Exactly, and what happened, usually, to the deposed kings? Or to claimants to the throne?

MORE. They were killed.

RICHARD. Which is why there was no outcry when Henry VII chopped off the head of the young Earl of Warwick, son of my brother Clarence, because he had a better claim to the throne than the Tudor. Henry VIII, your master, continued in this fine tradition. He executed anyone who had too much Plantagenet blood in their veins.

HISTORY. Objection, Your Honor. We are all familiar with the history of England. The defendant is trying to clear his name by comparing himself to others. I repeat, only Richard III is on trial here.

TIME. Sustained.

RICHARD. The point, Your Honor, that I would like to ask this historian, this Tudor historian, is this: are my alleged executions any worse than those of my predecessors or my successors?

MORE. In the light of accepted government policy of the time, no.

RICHARD. In your *History*, did you ever accuse me of killing my brother, the Duke of Clarence?

MORE. No, I merely said it was strongly *rumored* that you helped bring about his death.

RICHARD. In your *History,* did you write that I murdered King Henry VI who was my brother's prisoner in the Tower?

MORE. I repeated that which many men, living at the time, said was true.

RICHARD (*looking at ANNE*). Did you ever accuse me of killing my wife, Anne Neville?

MORE. Never.

RICHARD. And do you accuse me of ordering the deaths of my nephews, the Little Princes, again in the Tower?

MORE (*clearing his throat*). No one really knows for sure what was the fate of Edward V and his brother, the little Duke of York, and I said as much in my book.

RICHARD. It seems to me, good Sir Thomas, that your so-called *History of Richard III* was really written by Rumor and not you.

HISTORY and RUMOR (*rising together*). Objection!

TIME. Objection sustained. The jury will disregard the defendant's attempt to cast a shadow upon the reputation of this witness. (*HISTORY and RUMOR sit down.*)

RICHARD. Sir Thomas, you have already admitted that the policy of removing threats to the throne by death usually was silently accepted by the people, except, of course, in my case.

MORE (*evenly*). In my lifetime, I found the cares and matters of government policy too much for me and I voluntarily gave up my office as Lord Chancellor and retired to the peace of my home. If truth be known, I would rather be among the roses of my garden than among the Roses of Lancaster, York or Tudor. The former have less thorns.

RICHARD (*after a slight pause*). I have no more questions, Your Honor. (*He returns to his seat.*)

TIME. Then you may stand down, Sir Thomas.

MORE (*rises*). Thank you, Your Honor. (*He returns to his seat.*)

TIME. Call your next witness, Counselor.

HISTORY (*rising*). Your Honor, the prosecution calls William Shakespeare to the stand. (*There is a general buzz in the gallery.*)

BAILIFF. William Shakespeare, come into court! (*SHAKESPEARE rises from his seat and goes up to the witness stand. The BAILIFF swears him in.*) Do you swear to tell the truth, the whole truth, and nothing but the truth, so help you God?

SHAKESPEARE. I do. (*Sits as the BAILIFF withdraws. HISTORY comes center stage.*)

HISTORY. Please state your name and occupation for the record.

SHAKESPEARE. William Shakespeare of the Lord Chamberlain's Men, player and playwright.

HISTORY. Master Shakespeare, did you write any plays dealing with the defendant, Richard III?

SHAKESPEARE. Yes, I included his character in *Henry VI,* Parts 2 & 3 and, of course, *Richard III.*

HISTORY. Your Honor, at this time, I would like to introduce as evidence this copy of Master Shakespeare's play, *Richard III.* (*He picks up a modern playbook from his table and hands it to the JUDGE.*)

TIME. Does the defense have any objections?

CHARITY. No, Your Honor.

TIME. Very well. Clerk, please mark this playbook as Exhibit B. (*CLERK marks it and hands the book back to HISTORY.*)

HISTORY. Thank you. Now, Master Shakespeare, will you please examine this copy of your play, *Richard III*, and could you tell the court if it is, in fact, a true copy of your play as you wrote it. (*SHAKESPEARE takes the book and flips through the pages briefly.*)

SHAKESPEARE. The spelling is better and there are more stage directions, but the text is essentially correct. I must say, the printing and binding of this book is excellent. When I think what I could have done in my day with a word processor, instead of a quill pen!

HISTORY. Master Shakespeare, if we could return to the subject at hand? Where did you get your source material for this play of *Richard III*?

SHAKESPEARE. Chiefly from Raphael Holinshed's *Chronicles*, the 1587 edition.

HISTORY. And where did Holinshed get his material?

SHAKESPEARE. I believe from Thomas More's *History of Richard III*.

HISTORY. Do you respect these writers, Holinshed and More, as true historians?

SHAKESPEARE. Of course, they were both learned men, especially Thomas More. Why not?

HISTORY. Was there any objection to your treatment of Richard III?

SHAKESPEARE (*chuckling*). Certainly not from my audiences. They *loved* it. *Richard III* was one of my most popular plays. He was the villain everyone loved to hate.

CHARITY (*rising*). Objection! The witness is casting slurs upon my client.

TIME. Sustained. (*CHARITY sits down.*)

SHAKESPEARE. Sorry, Your Honor. I was merely telling you like it was.

HISTORY. Quite so. Now, in your play, did you write that Richard desired to wear the crown for himself?

SHAKESPEARE. Desired it?! He was *consumed* by it. That was the whole crux of my play. I think I established that very neatly in *Henry VI*, Part 3 in Richard's "to get the crown" speech.

HISTORY. And what did Richard do to "get the crown" as you so aptly put it?

SHAKESPEARE. To put it simply, he hacked his way to the throne.

CHARITY (*rising*). Objection! This has not been proved.

HISTORY. Your Honor, isn't this why we are all here in the first place? I am trying to prove this very point.

CHARITY. Counselor is putting words in the witness's mouth.

SHAKESPEARE (*aside*). Like a good playwright for players.

TIME. I will sustain the objection this time, but, Master History, phrase your questions more carefully.

HISTORY. Yes, Your Honor. Master Shakespeare, in your play, whom did you say Richard killed to "get the crown"?

CHARITY. Objection! These murders are alleged.

RUMOR. Aw, shut up and sit down, Charity, or we'll be here all day.

TIME. Objection overruled. I will permit the question, considering that the script has already been entered as evidence. Please answer the question, Master Shakespeare.

SHAKESPEARE. Well, let's see. Henry VI and his son, Edward, were already killed off before Act I. There's Clarence, Rivers, Vaughen, Grey, Hastings, the Little Princes, Queen Anne and Buckingham. I believe that's the lot.

RUMOR. That *is* quite a lot, if you ask me!

CHARITY (*aside*). Unfortunately, everyone does.

TIME (*banging the gavel*). Order!

HISTORY. In the 400 years since *Richard III* was written, has it been performed often?

SHAKESPEARE (*pleased*). Oh yes, indeed it has. All the greatest actors down through the years have portrayed my Richard - Burbage, Gerrick, Tree, Irving, Kemble, Olivier! (*Sighs.*) I only wish I could have enjoyed the royalties from their performances.

HISTORY. And so it would be safe to assume that your concept of Richard III based on the writings of More and Holinshed has been the most widely accepted?

SHAKESPEARE. I am pleased to think so - in all modesty.

HISTORY. Thank you, Master Shakespeare. I have no further questions. (*HISTORY sits as RICHARD rises and comes to the center.*)

RICHARD. William Shakespeare! At last we meet. Tell me, have you ever seen me before?

SHAKESPEARE. Of course not! I wasn't even born until 1564. You died years before that.

RICHARD. Exactly! As a matter of record, you were born 69 years after my death and you wrote your play about me 108 years after Bosworth Field. Is that not true?

SHAKESPEARE. Sounds about right.

RICHARD. Well then, Master Playwright, will you please tell the court, since you never saw me or met anyone who did, why you described me, and I quote: (*Reads from Exhibit B.*) "Love forswore me in my mother's womb: she did corrupt frail Nature with some bribe to shrink mine arm up like a withered shrub, to make an envious mountain on my back where sits deformity to mock my body, to shape my legs of an unequal size, to disproportion me in every part, like to a chaos, or an unlicked bear-whelp." You wrote this! Why?

SHAKESPEARE. I based my description on Sir Thomas More's - somewhat.

RICHARD. Somewhat!?

SHAKESPEARE (*getting uncomfortable*). Perhaps I took a few extra bits of poetic license.

RICHARD. You go on to write that I'm " ... valiant crook-back prodigy ... indigested and deformed bump ... bottled spider ... poisonous bunch-backed toad ... lump of foul deformity ... elvish-marked, abortive rooting hog!" *This* is poetic license? I'd call it slander, Sir Poet.

RUMOR (*rising*). Objection, Your Honor! Defense is badgering the witness. Besides, everyone knows what Richard III looked like.

RICHARD. They do? Do they really? Your Honor, may I continue this line of questioning?

TIME. I will allow you to do so, but curb your tone somewhat. Objection overruled.

RICHARD. Thank you, Your Honor. I will rephrase the question. Master Shakespeare, you see me here before you. Do I have a withered arm?

SHAKESPEARE. No.

RICHARD. Do I carry a hump on my back?

SHAKESPEARE. Not that I can perceive, although one shoulder does look higher than the other.

RICHARD. And finally, you see me walk. Do I limp or drag my foot along the ground as your actors do night after night upon the stage?

SHAKESPEARE. No, you walk very well.

COUNTESS OF DESMOND (*from her seat in the Gallery as an aside*). And he dances better than most, if truth be known. (*There is a ripple of comment in the Gallery.*)

TIME. Order! Who is that? Bailiff, bring the lady forward. (*BAILIFF escorts the COUNTESS to the center.*) Madam, what was the meaning of your outburst?

COUNTESS. Forgive me, Your Honor. I didn't realize my remark was spoken so loudly.

TIME. Who are you, Madam, for the record?

COUNTESS. I am the Countess of Desmond. I was a young girl in the court of the defendant's brother, Edward IV. It was my pleasure to dance with My Lord Richard on several occasions. As I was so young, no one had asked me to dance at the Christmas revels except the Duke of Gloucester, as he was known then. My, but did I hold my head high as I was led out to the floor on the arm of the King's favorite brother! He was always kind to me and to the other children at court. I thought he was the handsomest man in the room, except for his brother, the King, of course. Oh, yes, I remembered Richard long into my nineties when I was an honored lady in the court of the young Queen Elizabeth. I always spoke highly of him there. (*She sighs at the happy memory.*) Oh, my, yes!

HISTORY. Objection, Your Honor! As this lady has not been duly sworn and as she has spoken out of turn, the prosecution requests that this testimony be stricken from the record and the jury be instructed to disregard it.

TIME (*sighing*). Objection sustained and the jury is so instructed. Your Ladyship, the court thanks you for your show of loyalty to the defendant but I request you to return to your seat and forbear from further outbursts or I shall be forced to evict you from these proceedings.

COUNTESS. Of course, Your Honor, although I certainly didn't mean to be a bother to anyone.

RICHARD (*crossing quickly to the COUNTESS as she starts to return to her seat*). My lady, you were ever an ornament to my brother's court and your beauty has blossomed over the years. I am most grateful for your support. Please consider me always as your most humble servant. (*He kisses her hand. COUNTESS is delighted.*)

COUNTESS. Thank you, My Lord. (*She is escorted back to her seat as RUMOR rises.*)

RUMOR. Your Honor, these honeyed words we've just heard spoken by the defendant are perfect examples of how he *duped* the nobles and commons alike into accepting him as King! He convicts himself out of his own mouth!

TIME. Counselor, be seated. (*RUMOR is pulled down by HISTORY.*) The defense may continue the cross-examination.

RICHARD. Master Shakespeare, are you aware of my reputation as a soldier and a general. Did you know that I had been trained in warfare since the age of 9 by the Earl of Warwick? That I was fighting in combat at 16 and I fought by my brother's side at Tewkesbury when I was 18? And that I was appointed Warden of the Northern Marches against the Scottish by the time I was 20? Did you know all that?

SHAKESPEARE. I credited you with a good deal of courage, especially in your final speeches in Act V.

RICHARD. Then answer me this: if I had the deformities which you described again and again in your plays, how could I have possibly ridden a battle-charger and wielded a spear, sword and mace? I was an active, fighting soldier, not a general who sat behind on a hillside.

SHAKESPEARE (*a little testy*). Sir, I'm a writer. I write what I think will make a good play.

CHARITY (*rising*). Your Honor, at this point, the

defense requests that the slanderous description of my client be withdrawn from the record and furthermore, that the record show that Richard III to be of goodly shape, well-proportioned; and that he was an excellent soldier, a handsome man ... and a good dancer.

RUMOR. What about his shoulders? (*She also stands.*) All reports stated that one shoulder was higher than the other and that he was tiny in stature. I'd call that misshapen!

RICHARD. Your Honor, I was an average man's height and small-boned as was my father, the late Duke of York. In comparison with my brothers Edward, Edmond and George, all of whom were over 6 feet and broad-shouldered, I naturally looked smaller. In regard to my shoulders, I trained for long hours in my boyhood using the heavy arms of war. The muscles on my right arm and shoulder developed more than on the left and, on my bone structure, the difference was more obvious. But to say I was crook-backed is an odd way of describing a soldier's fighting physique.

HISTORY (*rising*). Your Honor, the prosecution will concede that there have been certain over-exaggerations of the defendant's personal looks and we will drop the matter. It is of no consequence, really, what Richard III looked like. We are more concerned with his actions. I suggest that the defense is trying to cloud the issue and to waste the court's time by dwelling on the minor accusation of ill-features.

TIME. I agree. The jury is henceforth to disregard any reference to the defendant's physical looks. Therefore, proceed with the matter at hand. Do you have any further questions of this witness?

RICHARD. I do, Your Honor. Now, Master Shakespeare, let us move to the heart of the matter - all those murders you give me dubious credit for.

SHAKESPEARE. I only wrote what I found in Holinshed and More. But you have to admit all those murders and power plays made a great drama. The audience loved it!

RICHARD. And who were your audiences?

SHAKESPEARE. Why, the people of London - merchants, apprentices, squires and the like. *Richard III* packed the Globe Theatre every time we performed it.

RICHARD. And at court?

SHAKESPEARE. At the court as well.

RICHARD. And whose court was it, Master Playwright, when you and your company performed?

SHAKESPEARE. That of our most Sovereign Lady, Queen Elizabeth.

RICHARD. Just so. Queen Elizabeth - the undoubted granddaughter of Henry VII, who, in former times, was the Earl of Richmond, Henry Tudor. Isn't that so? Queen Elizabeth was a Tudor?

SHAKESPEARE. Of course.

RICHARD. And so you wrote a Tudor history to please a Tudor queen?

SHAKESPEARE. No, not a history; merely a play. I wrote *Richard III* to entertain.

RICHARD. To entertain? And to be well paid for it, I presume?

SHAKESPEARE. Naturally. Actors have the same weaknesses everyone else has - they like to eat. If we perform a play that pleases, we are paid. The audiences come flocking. The theatre thrives and *we* thrive.

RICHARD. And who paid you when you played at court?

SHAKESPEARE. The Lord Chamberlain, of course.

RICHARD. Master Shakespeare, if you had written a play more sympathetic to me and showing Henry Tudor in his true colors, that is, as a remote claimant to the Throne who took my crown by force of arms, do you think your play would have been successful?

SHAKESPEARE. I think we all would have been thrown into the Tower if I had written the play as you suggest.

RICHARD. Why is that?

SHAKESPEARE. Very simply: such a play would have offended the good Lady on the throne and might have led to civil unrest. The Tudors ended 30 years of civil wars and Queen Elizabeth's reign was one of peace and prosperity. That's what the people of England wanted and that's what the Tudors's gave them and I, for one, wasn't about to bring up ethical questions concerning rights to the throne. History had already taken care of that. You were out; they were in and I wrote a play.

RICHARD. Henry Tudor killed my body on Bosworth Field in 1485, Master Shakespeare, but your play has been killing my soul for almost 400 years!

HISTORY. Objection! Defense is badgering the witness.

TIME. Sustained.

RICHARD. I beg the court's pardon, Your Honor. I have no further questions.

TIME. Witness may stand down. (*SHAKESPEARE returns to his seat as does RICHARD. HISTORY rises.*)

HISTORY. Your Honor, the prosecution has a number of other witnesses, all scholars, whose documented evidence points to the evil deeds of Richard III, however in the interest of time, we do not feel the need to bring them all forward. Our case is self-evident. The prosecution rests. (*Sits.*)

RUMOR (*aside to HISTORY*). Rests! How can you be so smug?

HISTORY. Relax, I know what I'm doing. Trust me!

CHARITY (*rising*). Your Honor, the defense calls Richard III to the Stand.

BAILIFF. Richard III, come into court!

RICHARD (*standing*). No need to shout. I'm already here. (*He goes up to the stand. BAILIFF swears him in.*)

BAILIFF. Do you swear to tell the truth, the whole truth and nothing but the truth, so help you God?

RICHARD. I do! (*He sits as the BAILIFF retires and CHARITY comes to center stage.*)

CHARITY. My Lord, please state your name and titles for the record.

RICHARD. I am Richard, Duke of Gloucester, afterward King Richard III. I am Lord High Admiral, Chief Constable of England, Warden of the Northern Marches, Knight of the Bath and Lord Protector of England. I am also the last Plantagenet, thanks to the Tudors.

HISTORY. Objection!

TIME. Sustained.

CHARITY. My Lord, will you tell the court briefly, and in your own words, your life prior to becoming king.

RICHARD. I was born during the period of English history known as the Wars of the Roses. When I was seven, I saw my home at Ludlow sacked and burned by the Lancasterian forces under Henry VI and many, many of my close friends were butchered. When I was nine, my father, the Duke of York, and my second brother, Edmund, were captured and executed by Henry's men. Edmund was only sixteen at the time. I was then sent to my cousin, the Earl of Warwick, in Middleham to become a squire in his household and to learn the arts of combat and warfare. Warwick taught us well. My three years at Middleham were the happiest of my life ... (*He pauses as he looks at his wife, ANNE NEVILLE, who smiles in return.*)

CHARITY (*gently*). And then, My Lord?

RICHARD. Then I was called to help my brother, Edward, now the king, fight the Lancastrians. He was truly the "Sun in splendor" which was the special device displayed on his shield. Edward could have been the best king England ever had, but Edward's weakness was for the ladies, especially his power-hungry wife, Elizabeth Woodville, and her army of relatives.

CHARITY. Yet you were loyal to Edward?

RICHARD. Always. I fought for him on the Scottish borders, in the western parts of England, and against the Lancastrians everywhere. I went into exile on the Continent with him. My motto is "Loyalty Binds me." I was loyal to Edward and to the Crown.

CHARITY. And your other brother, George, did he show this same loyalty?

RICHARD (*heatedly*). No, he did not! George looked out for one person only - himself. He was a bully, a glutton and he had an uncontrollable temper. He proved a traitor to England and to Edward time and time again.

CHARITY. Your Honor, at this time, the defense wishes

to present our evidence from the play *Richard III*, however, instead of merely reading the passages, we request that they be performed before the court. I understand that Master Shakespeare's company, the Lord Chamberlain's Men, are here and are, naturally, familiar with the script.

TIME. Does the prosecution have any objection to Counsel's suggestion?

HISTORY. None, Your Honor. In fact, we welcome such an opportunity.

RUMOR (*aside*). I can't believe it! She's even digging their own grave for them.

TIME. Bailiff, admit the players.

BAILIFF. Should they be sworn in, Your Honor?

TIME. No, they are merely performing a play and therefore are not called upon to tell the truth, so long as they remain faithful to the script.

RICHARD (*aside to CHARITY*). What are you doing? It's because of this foul play that my name and reputation have been blackened.

CHARITY. What better way can we prove your case than by questioning each scene and each event as it is depicted? If we can show how the play was an utter distortion of the truth, your case will be won.

RICHARD. I hope so.

CHARITY. Your Honor, and ladies and gentlemen of the jury, the play begins with a rather long soliloquy to show the character and motivation of Richard III. With your permission, the actors will present an abridged version.

TIME. You may begin.

(*PLAYER RICHARD - PR - comes to the center stage. He is wearing a prop crown.*)

PR. Now is the winter of our discontent made glorious summer by this sun of York . . .

RICHARD (*to himself*). My brother Edward - the sun in splendor.

PR. But I, that am not shaped for sportive tricks nor

made to court an amorous looking glass, cheated of feature by dissembling Nature, deformed, unfinished, sent before my time into this breathing world, scarce half made up, and that so lamely and unfashionable that dogs bark at me as I halt by them - And therefore, since I cannot prove a lover to entertain these fair, well-spoken days, I am determined to prove a villain and hate the idle pleasures of these days.

CHARITY. Your Honor, since we have already proved that Shakespeare's physical description of my client was false, we can, by logical inference, prove that the motive of envy is also false.

SHAKESPEARE (*from his seat*). I merely used a visual device to help the audience understand Richard's evil character. I got the idea from Thomas More. I mean, after all, a lot of my audience couldn't read!

TIME. Order!

PR (*to TIME*). Shall I continue, sir?

TIME. Please, proceed.

PR. Plots have I laid to set my brother Clarence and the King in deadly hate the one against the other. The King is sickly, weak and melancholy and his physicians fear for him mightily. He cannot live, I hope, but must not die till George be packed with post horses speedily up to heaven. I'll in, to urge his hatred more to Clarence with lies well-steeled, and, if I fail not in my deep intent, Clarence hath not another day to live: which done, God *take* King Edward to His mercy, and leave the world for *me* to bustle in! For then I'll marry Warwick's youngest daughter, what though I killed her husband and his father? (*PR steps to the side while CHARITY speaks.*)

CHARITY. My Lord, let us take the last accusation first. Did you kill Edward of Lancaster, then the husband of Anne Neville, Warwick's daughter?

RICHARD. I did not. Edward died in combat at the Battle of Tewkesbury in the spring of 1471. Yes, I was there on the opposite side but I did not strike him down in cold blood. I don't know whose sword thrust or arrow killed him. It was a heated battle. Incidentally,

Anne was only engaged to Edward, *not* his wife. The ceremony had not yet been performed.

CHARITY. Did you kill Henry VI in the Tower of London on May 21, 1471?

RICHARD. Henry VI was executed privately under direct order of my brother, King Edward IV. As Constable of England, I merely followed the orders of my King.

CHARITY. Shakespeare depicts you as wishing for Edward's death. Is this true?

RICHARD (*heatedly*). It's a lie! I had no idea my brother was dying. I was in the northern part of England at the time, guarding the borders. Edward died too soon. England needed him . . . and so did I.

CHARITY. Did you stir up hatred between your brothers Edward, the King, and George, Duke of Clarence?

RICHARD. No, Clarence managed to do that all by himself. He was disloyal to Edward and fought against him. Eventually he was captured and was tried before the House of Lords in Parliament for treason against the crown.

CHARITY. Your Honor, I have here the accusations drawn up against the Duke of Clarence at his trial. This is a copy of the official records of Parliament from February 1478. I would like to enter them as evidence for the defense.

TIME. Does the prosecution have any objection?

HISTORY (*rising*). Your Honor, this isn't the trial of George, Duke of Clarence. I see no point in submitting the charges against him into this court. May I remind us all that we are trying his brother, Richard?

CHARITY. Your Honor, I wish to make the point that Clarence was legally tried and convicted of treason and that his death was a legal execution.

TIME. I overrule your objection, History, and will admit the document. Clerk, please mark it as Exhibit C. (*CLERK marks it as HISTORY sits down in a huff.*)

CHARITY. Thank you, Your Honor. Now, My Lord, will you please read aloud the last two charges for the court?

RICHARD (*taking the paper and reading*). "...that he, Clarence, did break the King's peace and levied war against the King in Cambridge and Huntingdonshire and that he, Clarence, charged the King to be a bastard and himself, Clarence, to be the true and rightful King of England." (*There is a low murmur in the Gallery section.*)

CHARITY. And what was the verdict in Clarence's case?

RICHARD. Guilty of treason against the King.

CHARITY. And the sentence?

RICHARD. Death by hang, drawn and quartering.

CHARITY. Did you sign the death warrant?

RICHARD. No, only the King can do that. Edward IV signed the warrant against his own brother. (*Another murmur in the Gallery.*)

CHARITY. And was the traitor's death carried out on Clarence?

RICHARD. No, he was executed privately in the Tower.

CHARITY. Your Honor, at this time, I would request the players to enact the death of Clarence as Shakespeare wrote it.

TIME. Granted.

(*PR returns to center stage as the two players enacting the MURDERERS rise from their seats and come forward.*)

PR. But, soft! Here come my executioners. How now, my hardy, stout, resolved mates! Are you going to dispatch this thing?

MURDERER ONE. We are, my lord, and come to have the warrant, that we may be admitted where he is.

PR. Well thought upon; I have it here about me. (*Gives them the warrant.*) But, sirs, be sudden in the execution. Do not hear him plead, for Clarence is well-spoken and, perhaps, may move your hearts to pity if you mark him.

MURDERER TWO. Tut, tut, my lord! We will not stand to prate. We go to use our hands, and not our tongues.

PR. I like you, lads: about your business straight. Go, go, dispatch.

MURDERER ONE. We will, my noble lord. (*PR returns to his seat as the MURDERERS move to one side.*)

(*CLARENCE enters and lies downstage and sleeps. BRACKENBURY enters and speaks to the audience.*)

BRACKENBURY (*regarding the sleeping CLARENCE*). Sorrow breaks seasons and reposing hours. Princes have but their titles for their glories, so that between their title and a low name there's nothing differs but the outward fame. (*MURDERERS come forward.*)

MURDERER ONE. Ho! Who's here?

BRACKENBURY (*surprised*). What wouldst thou, fellow?

MURDERER ONE. I would speak with Clarence.

MURDERER TWO. Let him see our commission, and talk no more. (*MURDERER ONE gives BRACKENBURY the warrant.*)

BRACKENBURY (*looking over the warrant*). I am, in this, commanded to deliver the Noble Duke of Clarence to your hands. I will not reason what is meant hereby. (*Points to the sleeping CLARENCE.*) There lies the Duke, asleep, and there the keys. (*Hands keys to MURDERER ONE.*) I'll to the King and signify to him that thus I have resigned to you my charge.

MURDERER ONE (*taking keys*). You may, sir, 'tis a point of wisdom. Fare you well. (*BRACKENBURY exits as the two MURDERERS come up to CLARENCE.*)

MURDERER TWO (*as MURDERER ONE draws knife*). Shall we stab him as he sleeps?

MURDERER ONE. No. He'll say 'twas done cowardly, when he wakes.

MURDERER TWO. Why, he shall never wake until the great Judgement Day.

MURDERER ONE. Why, *then* he'll say we stabbed him sleeping.

MURDERER TWO (*stepping back*). The urging of that word "judgement" hath bred a kind of remorse in me.

MURDERER ONE. Remember our reward when the deed's done.

MURDERER TWO. Come, he dies! I had forgot the reward.

MURDERER ONE. Where's thy conscience now?

MURDERER TWO. O, in the Duke of Gloucester's purse.

RICHARD. Lies! I *never* hired assassins to murder Clarence!

TIME. Order! Proceed.

MURDERER TWO. Come, shall we fall to work?

MURDERER ONE. Take him on the costard with the hilts of thy sword, and then throw him into the malmsey butt in the next room.

MURDERER TWO (*laughing*). O excellent device! and make a sop of him.

MURDERER ONE. Soft! He wakes. (*CLARENCE stirs.*)

MURDERER TWO (*pulling out his knife*). Strike!

CLARENCE (*waking*). Where art thou, Keeper. Give me a cup of wine.

RICHARD (*aside*). *That* part is true enough!

MURDERER TWO. You shall have wine enough, my lord, anon.

CLARENCE (*looking at the MURDERERS and suddenly realizing who they are*). In God's name, what art thou? Thy voice is thunder, but thy looks are humble.

MURDERER ONE. My voice is now the King's, my looks mine own.

MURDERER TWO. Therefore, my lord, prepare to die.

CLARENCE. What is my offense? Where is the evidence that doth accuse me? Or who pronounced the bitter sentence of poor Clarence's death?

MURDERER ONE. What we do, we do upon command.

MURDERER TWO. And he that hath commanded is our king.

RICHARD (*aside*). *That* also is true!

CLARENCE. I will send you to my brother Gloucester who shall reward you better for my life than Edward will for tidings of my death.

MURDERER TWO. You are deceived. Your brother
Gloucester hates you.

CLARENCE (*panicked*). O no! He loves me and holds me
dear!

MURDERER ONE. Right, as snow in harvest. Come,
you deceive yourself. 'Tis he that sends us to destroy
you here.

CLARENCE (*more panicked*). It cannot be, for he
bewept my fortune and swore with sobs that he would
labor my delivery.

RICHARD (*rising*). I did! I did! I pleaded with Edward to
spare him!

RUMOR. Crying crocodile tears all the while, no doubt.

RICHARD. That's a lie!

TIME (*banging the gavel*). Order! Order! Counselors,
speak to your collegues, or I'll hold you *all* in
contempt of court!

HISTORY (*pulling RUMOR back down to her seat*).
Pardon, Your Honor.

CHARITY (*motioning to RICHARD to sit, which he does*).
It will not happen again, sir.

TIME (*to the PLAYERS*). Continue.

MURDERER ONE. Why so he doth, when he delivers
you from this earth's thralldom to the joys of heaven.

MURDERER TWO. Make peace with God for you must
die, my lord.

MURDERER ONE (*stabbing CLARENCE from behind*).
Take that! and that! If all this will not do, I'll drown
you in the malmsey butt within. (*Drags the body back
to the Gallery where the TWO PLAYERS return to their
seats.*)

MURDERER TWO. A bloody deed, and desperately
dispatched! How fain, like Pilate, would I wash my
hands of this most grievous murder! (*Returns to his
seat.*)

CHARITY (*coming to center again*). This is how Master
Shakespeare presented Clarence's death. You have
stated it is not true?

RICHARD. None of it. In Edward's mercy, Clarence was
given the choice of execution. His mind had become

unstable under the pressure of imprisonment. He chose the best and easiest death he could think of in his wild fantasies. He died by being drowned in a butt of malmsey wine, not stabbed.

CHARITY. For the record, my lord, how many gallons does a wine butt hold?

RICHARD. 126. My foolish brother, George, literally drank himself to death!

RUMOR (*aside*). What a waste of good wine!

CHARITY. And this was Clarence's choice?

RICHARD. It was and it was duly carried out and witnessed as a legal execution. I had no hand in it.

CHARITY. My lord, let us move along to the next series of events. Your brother, Edward IV, died of a stroke April 9, 1483, leaving as his heir twelve-year-old Edward, now Edward V. Can you tell us what happened then?

RICHARD. The King's death was sudden and the country, as well as the family, were taken by surprise. I was in the North and was *not* informed of Edward's death for over a week.

CHARITY. Why was.this?

RICHARD (*bitterly*). My brother, at the age of nineteen, married a commoner, a widow by the name of Elizabeth Woodville. The new Queen not only had two sons by her first marriage, but six sisters and five brothers who seemed insatiable for power and position. Edward IV showered land, offices, titles and revenues on all of them. They always wanted more and more. They flattered Edward and indulged him in his appetites for idleness and pleasures while they, the Woodvilles, ruled through the Queen. When the King died, he left me as the Lord Protector of the young Prince Edward, *not* the Queen's relatives. The boy was at Ludlow near Wales at the time with his uncle, Lord Rivers, who was the Queen's brother, and with his half-brother, Richard Grey. The Woodvilles knew, as I knew, whoever controlled the Prince would control the country. The Woodvilles wanted the power and they wanted me out.

CHARITY. So there was no love between you and your brother's in-laws?

RICHARD (*heatedly*). Never! They were a scheming pack of vulgar, power-mad upstarts...

HISTORY. Objection!

RICHARD. ...who wanted the throne of England for themselves!

HISTORY (*rising*). Objection!

TIME. Sustained. The jury will disregard the defendant's last remarks. (*HISTORY sits.*)

RICHARD. To answer your question why I was not told of the King's death, it was simply that the Queen-widow and her family wanted Prince Edward in London and crowned as quickly as possible before I had any knowledge of these events.

CHARITY. Why?

RICHARD. I feared for England. I had worked, and fought and braved exile since I was fourteen years old for England's sake. I wasn't going to stand by and watch her ruin at the hands of the Queen's grasping relatives. My brother entrusted the Prince to *me*, not to the Queen, nor to her brother, Lord Rivers.

CHARITY. Then what happened? What did you do?

RICHARD. I rode down from the North with my men and intercepted the young Prince's party at Northampton. There I had Lord Rivers and Richard Grey arrested for treason.

CHARITY. Treason? Please explain to the court.

RICHARD. It was treason to try to circumvent the late King's will by keeping both his death and the whereabouts of the heir a secret from the appointed Lord Protector. *I* was responsible for Prince Edward. In effect, Lord Rivers kidnapped him. *That* is treason in my book.

RUMOR (*aside*). But is it in the law book?

RICHARD. I arrested Rivers, Grey and Thomas Vaughen, who was also a part of this conspiracy, and had them taken to Pontefract. There they were beheaded.

CHARITY. For the crime of treason?

RICHARD. Yes, on my order as Lord Protector of England. Meanwhile the Queen, though often given to dramatic hysterical outbursts, was clear-thinking enough to go into sanctuary at Westminster.

CHARITY. What do you mean by the term "clear-thinking"?

RICHARD. She not only took her children, but also all the treasure and furnishings of the palace that she could lay her hands on. She even took the Great Seal of England with her as well as the jewels from the Tower. They weren't hers, but mine, by right, and she knew it!

HISTORY. Objection! Whatever the Queen took with her into sanctuary was her own property.

TIME. Sustained. Counselor, the hour is almost up. Be brief in your questioning.

CHARITY. I will, Your Honor. My lord, did you kill your nephews, known as the Little Princes?

RICHARD. I did not!

CHARITY. Did you kill your wife, Anne Neville?

RICHARD. No, how could I? (*He looks over to where ANNE is sitting.*) She was the one person who loved me for myself. And I loved her with all my heart. Of all the lies that Shakespeare depicted, this one is the worst. Anne died of consumption - you'd call it tuberculosis - in March of 1485. My heart died with her. Five months later, Henry Tudor killed what was left of me on Bosworth Field.

CHARITY. Thank you, my lord. I have no further questions. (*She sits as HISTORY rises and comes to center stage.*)

TIME. Counselor, you may cross-examine the defendant.

HISTORY. You stated that as Lord Protector you were responsible for the young king at the request of the late king. Under the terms of Edward IV's will, how long would you have remained Lord Protector?

RICHARD. Until the day the Prince was crowned king. It was my intention to request that Parliament appoint me as Regent during the Prince's minority.

HISTORY. So, in fact, your tenure as Lord Protector would have lasted a month or two at the most?

RICHARD. Under the existing terms of the will. Once Prince Edward was crowned, he would be under complete control of his mother's grasping family.

HISTORY. Leaving you out in the cold since you bore an open dislike for the Woodvilles, as you yourself have admitted. You never intended the young king to rule, did you? From the moment you heard of your brother's death, you plotted to take the throne for yourself, didn't you?

CHARITY. Objection! Prosecution is leading the witness.

TIME. Sustained. The jury will disregard the last question.

HISTORY. Since we have already mentioned the young king, Edward V, let us proceed to the most infamous crime of your career, the death of the Little Princes in the Tower. (*Pauses.*) Your Honor, may I approach the bench for a private word?

TIME. You may. Charity, approach the bench as well. (*Both COUNSELORS come forward and speak to TIME in low voices.*)

HISTORY. Your Honor, the mother of the Princes, Queen Elizabeth, is here in court. She may find my cross-examination very painful. Perhaps it would be in her best interests to leave while I question the defendant.

CHARITY. I agree, Your Honor. The Queen does become quite upset easily.

TIME. The court thanks you both for your tact and understanding. (*COUNSELORS return to their places.*) Queen Elizabeth, please rise.

QUEEN (*standing*). Here, Your Honor.

TIME. My lady, the prosecution intends to question the defendant in detail concerning the deaths of your sons, Edward and Richard, and has suggested that you would find these proceedings too painful. Therefore, you may leave the court at this time.

QUEEN. No, Your Honor. I'll *not* leave. I have waited

too long for this. The blood of my murdered sons cries out for justice and I intend to see justice to be done!

TIME. Very well, my lady, but you must control yourself or you will be evicted by the bailiff.

QUEEN. I understand, Your Honor. (*She sits as CHARITY also returns to her seat and HISTORY crosses down to the witness.*)

HISTORY. Your Honor, I request the Lord Chamberlain's Men to enact the scenes pertaining to the Little Princes. My worthy opponent should have no objections as she introduced the players in the first place.

TIME. Very well. Proceed.

(*Enter from the Gallery PR and PRINCE EDWARD.*)

PRINCE. Uncle Gloucester, if our brother come, where shall we sojourn till our coronation?

PR. Where it seems best unto your royal self. If I may counsel you, some day or two Your Highness shall repose you in the Tower; then where you please, and shall be thought most fit for your best health and recreation.

PRINCE. I do not like the Tower, of any place.

PR (*aside*). So wise so young, they say, do never live long.

PRINCE. What say you, Uncle?

PR. I say, without historical records, fame lives long.

HISTORY. Why did you put the Prince into the Tower upon his arrival in London?

RICHARD. You know yourself that it is the time-honored custom for rulers to reside in the Tower before they are crowned. The Tower is not just a prison, but contains many fine and comfortable apartments and is still considered a Royal Residence. Besides, there was no place else for the prince to go, his mother having fled into sanctuary.

HISTORY. Because she was afraid of you!

RICHARD. Because she realized that her power over the throne was ended and that I would not tolerate her

meddling into the affairs of state as she and her family
had done during my brother's reign.

QUEEN (*rising*). I feared for my life!

TIME. Order! Prosecutor, I hold you responsible for these
outbursts! (*QUEEN sits*.)

HISTORY. Forgive me, Your Honor. We will proceed.
Players, continue.

(*Enter RICHARD, DUKE OF YORK with BUCKINGHAM*.)

BUCKINGHAM. Now, in good time, here comes the
Duke of York.

PRINCE (*greeting YORK*). Richard of York, how fares
our noble brother?

YORK. Well, my dread lord - so must I call you now.

PRINCE (*sadly*). Ay, brother, to our grief as it is yours.

PR (*to YORK*). How fares our cousin, noble Lord of
York?

YORK. I thank you, gentle uncle. (*Looking at the
PRINCE*.) O my lord, you said that idle weeds are fast
in growth: the prince my brother hath outgrown me
far.

PR. He hath, my lord.

YORK (*teasing*). And therefore is he idle?

PR. O my fair cousin, I must not say so.

YORK. Then he is more beholding to you than I.

PR. He may command me as my sovereign. But you have
power in me as in a kinsman. My lord, will't please
you pass along? Myself and my good cousin
Buckingham will to your mother, to entreat her to
meet you at the Tower and welcome you.

YORK (*to the PRINCE, dismayed*). What, will you go
unto the Tower, my lord?

PRINCE. My Lord Protector needs have it so.

YORK. I shall not sleep in quiet at the Tower.

PR. Why, what should you fear?

YORK. Marry, my uncle Clarence's angry ghost: my
granddam told me he was murdered there.

PRINCE. I fear no uncles - dead.

PR. Nor none that live, I hope.

PRINCE (*meaningfully*). And if they live, I hope I need not fear. (*To YORK*.) But come, my lord, and with a heavy heart, thinking on them, go I unto the Tower. (*They exit into the Gallery with BUCKINGHAM*.)

PR (*to audience*). O 'tis a clever boy. He is all the mother's, from top to toe. (*He returns to his seat*.)

QUEEN (*aside*). Oh, my poor babes!

HISTORY. Since you already had the young king Edward in your control, why did you deem it necessary to take his brother, nine-year-old Richard, from his mother in sanctuary to be with his older brother?

RICHARD. To begin with, I didn't *take* Richard away from his mother; she let him go. His brother, Edward, was alone. His Woodville relatives were all arrested and proven traitors and his mother refusing to come out of sanctuary, he needed someone whom he knew and loved to be with him.

HISTORY. What about you? You were his uncle, weren't you? Didn't he love and trust you?

RICHARD. He hardly knew me. I had lived most of the time in the north and Prince Edward had been in his own household at Ludlow for several years. We hardly ever met.

HISTORY. I submit, my lord, that you wanted not only the new king but his heir, his brother Richard, under your control. Once they were out of the way, you had sole claim to the throne.

CHARITY. Objection!

RICHARD. Ridiculous! There were Prince Edward's five sisters as well as Clarence's children ahead of me! Also, I would like to point out that there was a question of the legality of my brother's marriage to Elizabeth Woodville. He had been pre-contracted to the Lady Elenor Butler and that pre-contract was never cancelled. Thus all the children by the Queen were bastards in the eyes of the law and of the Church and therefore the Little Princes could not inherit the crown. This was proclaimed in Parliament in early July 1483.

TIME. Objection sustained.

HISTORY (*sighs*). Very well, let us go on to the next scene, players.

(*PLAYER QUEEN - PQ and the PLAYER ANNE - PA rise from their seats and come center.*)

PA. God give your Grace a happy and joyful time of day!

PQ. As much to you, good sister. Whither away?

PA. No further than the Tower, and, as I guess, upon the same devotion as yourself, to see the gentle princes there.

PQ. Kind sister, thanks. We'll enter together. (*BRACKENBURY appears.*) And in good time, here the Lieutenant comes. Master Lieutenant, pray you, by your leave, how doth the Prince, and my young son of York?

BRACKENBURY. Right well, dear madam. By your patience, I may not suffer you to visit them; the King hath strict charged the contrary.

PQ. The King? Who's that?

BRACKENBURY. I mean the Lord Protector.

PQ. The Lord protect him from that kingly title! Hath he set bounds between their love and me? I am their mother; who shall bar me from them?

BRACKENBURY. No, madam, no! I may not leave it so: I am bound by oath, and therefore pardon me. (*Exits.*)

PA. Go thou to sanctuary, and good thoughts possess thee!

PQ. Stay, yet look back with me unto the Tower. Pity, you ancient stones, those tender babes whom envy hath immured within your walls, rough cradle for such little pretty ones! Rude, ragged nurse, old sullen playfellow for tender princes, use my babies well! So foolish sorrow bids your stones farewell. (*PA and PQ return to their seats in the Gallery.*)

RICHARD. This scene was a lie from start to finish! To begin with, my wife, the Lady Anne, was not in London at the time. Secondly, never *once* did the

Queen try to visit the Princes. If she had, she could have seen them! I gave no order to stop her.

QUEEN (*rising*). I wanted to! I would have but I was afraid of what that ... that villain would do to me, if I fell into his clutches!

TIME. Order!

CHARITY. Your Honor, since this scene is so obviously false, even by the admission of the Dowager Queen, the defense moves that the jury be instructed to disregard it. This scene is calculated to play upon their emotions in a manner not sympathetic to my client.

SHAKESPEARE (*also rising*). That was the whole point of that scene! Weeping mothers make great theatre!

TIME (*banging the gavel*). Order! Bailiff, see that Master Shakespeare remains seated and quiet. So too the Queen Mother. Mistress Charity, I will so rule upon this scene as the defense requests. The jury is instructed to disregard it. (*SHAKESPEARE and the QUEEN sit.*)

HISTORY. Very well, Your Honor, we will proceed to the next one - a scene that will cast no shadow of doubt as to the defendant's guilt. (*PR and BUCKINGHAM come to the center.*)

PR. Ah, Buckingham, young Edward lives. Think now what I would speak.

BUCKINGHAM. Say on, my lord.

PR. Why, Buckingham, I say I would be king.

BUCKINGHAM. Why, so you are, my thrice-renowned liege.

PR. Ha? Am I king? 'Tis so. But Edward lives.

BUCKINGHAM. True, noble Prince.

PR. O bitter consequence, that Edward still should live true noble Prince! Cousin, thou wast not wont to be so dull. Shall I be plain? I wish the bastards *dead*, and I would have it suddenly performed. What sayest thou now? Speak suddenly, be brief.

BUCKINGHAM (*taken aback*). Give me some little breath, some pause, dear Lord, before I positively speak in this: I will resolve you herein presently. (*Exits.*)

PR. The deep-revolving witty Buckingham no more shall be the neighbor to *my* counsels. (*He steps to the side.*)

HISTORY. You afterward proclaimed the Duke of Buckingham a traitor and had *his* head chopped off. Wasn't that because he refused to kill the Little Princes for you?

RICHARD. No, it was because he tried to join forces with the upstart Henry Tudor against me. I'd call anyone a traitor who takes sides against the lawful king.

HISTORY. But he joined the Tudor faction because he wished to have nothing more to do with you, didn't he?

RICHARD. He felt I owed him money and lands for his support for me against the Woodvilles. He wanted too much. I refused to give in to his demands and he defected. Even Shakespeare had him admit this later in the scene. His treachery had nothing to do with the Little Princes.

HISTORY. Players, continue on to the next scene!

(*Enter TYRREL.*)

PR (*stepping back to center*). Is thy name Tyrrel?

TYRREL (*bowing*). James Tyrrel, and your most obedient subject.

PR. Art thou indeed? Darest thou resolve to kill a friend of mine?

TYRREL. Please you; but I had rather kill two enemies.

PR. Why then thou hast it! Two deep enemies, foes to my rest and my sweet sleep's disturbers. Tyrrel, I mean those bastards in the Tower.

TYRREL. Let me have open means to come to them, and soon I'll rid you from fear of them.

PR. Thou sayest sweet music. Hark, come hither, Tyrrel, and lend thine ear. (*Whispers to him, then gives him a ring.*) Go, by this token.

TYRREL (*putting on the ring*). I will dispatch it straight. (*They return to the Gallery and sit.*)

HISTORY. Your Honor, in the *History of Richard III*,

written by Thomas More and which is already entered as evidence, the illustrious author names James Tyrrel as the murderer of the Princes at Richard's command.

CHARITY. Objection, Your Honor, may I remind the court that by Sir Thomas' own admission, the manuscript was garbled and incomplete and we have shown that it also contains errors.

TIME. Sustained.

HISTORY. Your Honor, in the reign of Henry VII, nineteen years after the fact, James Tyrrel confessed to his part in this heinous crime.

CHARITY. May I remind the court that James Tyrrel made this alleged "confession" while under sentence of death for his supposed *Yorkist* leanings? Furthermore, Tyrrel was executed privately and without trial by Henry VII - an action that my client is currently charged with.

TIME. The court will weigh all these arguments, counselors. Have you any more questions of this witness, Master History?

HISTORY. May it please the court to see the final scene of the murder of the Little Princes?

TIME. Continue.

HISTORY. Players, finish the act. (*TYRREL comes to the center.*)

TYRREL. The tyrannous and bloody act is done; the most arch deed of piteous massacre that ever yet this land was guilty of. Dighton and Forrest, (*The two MURDERERS come one on each side of TYRREL.*) who I did suborn to do this piece of ruthless butchery wept like to children in their death's sad story.

DIGHTON. O thus lay the gentle babes.

FORREST. Thus, thus girdling one another within their innocent arms. Their lips were four red roses on a stalk, and in their summer beauty kissed each other. A book of prayers on their pillow lay, which once almost changed my mind. But ...O, the Devil!

DIGHTON. We smothered the most replenished sweet work of nature that from prime creation ever she framed. (*QUEEN begins to weep softly at first, then more loudly.*)

TYRREL. They could speak no more and so I left them both to bear this tidings to the bloody King.

(*The two MURDERERS return to their seats as TYRREL steps to one side. Meanwhile the QUEEN rises and comes forward in a great display of emotion.*)

QUEEN. Oh, oh, horrible! My sons, my babies. Never were there two sweeter, more gentle boys than mine!

TIME. Order!

QUEEN (*pointing to RICHARD*). And you! You devil, you *killed* them! Why? They never harmed you. Why?

TIME (*banging the gavel*). Order! Bailiff!

QUEEN (*tries to strike RICHARD but is held back by the BAILIFF*). Murderer! Murderer! Smothered in the night! To die without a prayer on their lips! You should burn for ten thousand years in the deepest pit of Hell! Murderer! (*BAILIFF slaps the QUEEN who then breaks down crying.*)

TIME. Bailiff, please escort the Queen from court. My Lady Countess of Desmond, if you would be so good as to accompany Her Majesty. (*BAILIFF and COUNTESS help the QUEEN off the stage. BAILIFF returns during the following speech.*) Master History, is there any more you wish to present to the court before excusing the witness?

HISTORY. One final scene, Your Honor. Players, conclude!

(*TYRREL returns to center as PR comes down from Gallery.*)

TYRREL. And here he comes. (*Bows.*) All health, my sovereign lord!

PR. Kind Tyrrel, am I happy in thy news?

TYRREL. If to have done the thing you gave in charge beget your happiness, be happy then, for it is done.

PR. But didst thou see them dead?

TYRREL. I did, my lord.

PR. And buried, gentle Tyrrel?

TYRREL. The chaplain of the Tower hath buried them; but where, to say the truth, I do not know. (*PR and TYRREL return to the Gallery and sit*.)

HISTORY. My lord, I ask you plainly: did you commission James Tyrrel or any man to murder Edward V and his brother sometime in August of 1483?

RICHARD. No, I did not. This scene shows me to be in London at the time. That is in error. Queen Anne, my wife, and I were at Warwick on Royal Progress in August.

HISTORY. When the rumors of the Princes' deaths spread, why didn't you produce the boys for the people to see?

RICHARD. That was my intention but I discovered it was too late; the boys were already dead. (*Murmur in the Gallery*.)

HISTORY. Who killed them?

RICHARD. I don't know. Either it was someone who thought he was doing me a favor or an enemy who wanted to make me look the arch-villain.

RUMOR. Which you are, in truth!

HISTORY. You sit there and fully expect this court to believe that the Little Princes, who were supposedly under your *protection* in that huge stone fortress known as the Tower, were killed by a person or persons unknown? Why didn't you publicly announce their murders and lead a search for the killers?

RICHARD. As you say, the Princes were in my protection. Who would believe me if I announced that they had been killed while in my safekeeping but I didn't do it? Would the good citizens of London believe me that I didn't know *who* had killed them? Would I be trusted to keep England safe if I couldn't even keep my own nephews from harm? Perhaps I should have made a big show in hunting down the murderers. Who knows?

RUMOR. Tyrrel knew.

RICHARD. Did he? Or did he merely confess in the hopes of saving his own skin by proving he was working for Henry Tudor's interests all along? Tyrrel was no stranger to me, as the play indicates. He was one of my henchmen who later found it more convenient to uphold the claim of the Tudors. Many did. Lord Stanly, the Earl of Derby, did by turning his colors at Bosworth Field. His treacherous action cost me my crown and my life.

RUMOR. They say that the night before your final battle, you had a restless night, haunted by dreams of those whom you had murdered.

RICHARD (*losing patience*). Show me one general who sleeps soundly the night before a major battle and I'll show you a liar or an idiot. It *is* true I was wakeful but I was *not* haunted by dreams or ghosts.

HISTORY. Players, enact the scene we speak of.

(*PR comes to the center and lies down and sleeps. The GHOSTS enter, one by one, from the Gallery and stand in a semicircle behind the restless PR. First, enter the GHOST OF EDWARD OF LANCASTER.*)

EDWARD. Let me sit heavy on thy soul tomorrow! Think how thou stabbest me in my prime of youth at Tewkesbury; despair therefore and die!

CHARITY. Your Honor, we have already proven this accusation false.

(*Enter the GHOST OF HENRY VI.*)

HENRY VI. When I was mortal, my anointed body by thee was punched full of deadly holes. Think on the Tower and me; despair and die!

CHARITY. Henry VI's death was at the express command of Edward IV, not my client, Your Honor.

(*Enter the GHOST OF CLARENCE.*)

CLARENCE. Let me sit heavy in thy soul tomorrow. I, that was washed to death with fulsome wine, poor Clarence by thy guile betrayed to death!

CHARITY. This death, too, was ordered by Edward IV as a lawful execution for treason, as we have shown earlier.

(*Enter the GHOSTS OF THE LITTLE PRINCES.*)

PRINCE. Dream on thy cousins smothered in the Tower.

YORK. Let us be lead within thy bosom, Richard, and weigh thee down to ruin, shame and death!

CHARITY. You have all heard my client testify under oath that he did not kill his nephews but that they died without his knowledge or consent.

RUMOR. Since when did a mere oath stop Richard III?

(*Enter the GHOST OF QUEEN ANNE.*)

PA. Richard, thy wife, that wretched Anne thy wife, that never slept a quiet hour with thee, now fills *thy* sleep with perturbations. Tomorrow in the battle, think on me and fall that edgeless sword: despair and die!

ALL GHOSTS. Despair and die! (*They back off and melt back into the Gallery as they chant.*) Despair and die! Despair and die! (*PR awakes with a start, gets up and returns to his seat as RICHARD rises in anger.*)

RICHARD. Now, by heaven, I have had enough! I can sit by and listen to you all lie and slander my name with alleged crimes, but this last is too much! You *won't* slander the good name of my wife - not in this court!

TIME. *Order*! Counselor, have you any *further* questions of the defendant?

HISTORY. No, Your Honor, not at this time. I feel that this last outburst has shown Richard III in his true colors. (*He returns to his seat.*)

TIME (*with some relief*). The defendant can step down. (*RICHARD returns to his seat.*) Does the defense have any more witnesses?

CHARITY. I have one more, Your Honor. I would like to call Queen Anne, wife of Richard III, to the stand.

BAILIFF. Queen Anne, come into court.

RICHARD (*aside to CHARITY*). My wife's health has always been delicate. Please don't tax her strength.

CHARITY. I will be brief.

(*ANNE comes to the witness stand.*)

BAILIFF. Do you swear to tell the truth, the whole truth, and nothing but the truth, so help you God?

ANNE. I do. (*She sits.*)

CHARITY. Please state your name and title for the record.

ANNE. I am Anne Neville, younger daughter of the late Earl of Warwick, and am wife of Richard III and Queen of England.

CHARITY. My lady, how long have you known your husband?

ANNE. Almost all my life. I was five years old when Richard came as a boy to my father's castle at Middleham for schooling. He was nine then.

CHARITY. And when did you fall in love with him?

ANNE (*with a gentle smile*). I can't remember when exactly. I always admired him and that admiration slowly turned to love. I used to watch him from the upper windows when he was in the tilt yard. He was always kind and gentle with me. He never teased me like the other boys who were also in training.

CHARITY. You have heard your husband accused in open court of murders and infamous conduct, do you believe him to be guilty as charged?

ANNE. No, never! He was very upset over the death of the Duke of Clarence and when he, in the course of fighting in the field or as a king, found it necessary to kill, he did so with a great deal of reluctance. But I know he could never murder anyone in cold blood, especially not the Little Princes! They were Family and in his protection.

CHARITY. My lady, Shakespeare in his play *Richard III* presents you as a most unwilling wife to Richard. Is this true?

ANNE (*angrily*). No! It is false through and through!

CHARITY. Your Honor, if it will please the court, I would request the Players to enact the scene of Richard's courtship for the jury.

TIME. Has the prosecution any objection?

HISTORY. No, Your Honor.

TIME. Very well, proceed.

(*Enter PA accompanied by two of the PLAYERS bearing the covered body of HENRY VI.*)

PA. Set down, set down your honorable load whilst I awhile lament the untimely fall of virtuous Lancaster. Poor key-cold figure of a holy king, hear the lamentations of poor Anne, wife to thy Edward, to thy slaughtered son stabbed by the selfsame hand that mocks these wounds! O cursed be the hand that made these holes! Curse the heart that had the heart to do it! If ever he have a wife, let her be made more miserable by the death of him than I am made by my young lord and thee! (*To the BEARERS.*) Come, now towards Chertsy with your holy load. (*PR comes center stage.*)

PR (*stopping the BEARERS*). Stay, you that bear the corpse and set it down.

PA. What black magician conjure up this fiend, to stop devoted charitable deeds?

PR. Sweet saint, for charity, be not so ill-tempered.

PA. Foul devil, for God's sake, hence, and trouble us not for thou hast made the happy earth thy hell.

PR. Lady, you know no rules of charity, which renders good for bad, blessings for curses.

PA. Villain, thou knowest no law of God nor man: no beast so fierce but knows some touch of pity.

PR. But I know none, and therefore am no beast.

PA. Oh, wonderful, when Devils tell the truth!

PR. More wonderful, when angels are so angry! I did not kill your husband.

PA (*sarcastically*). Why, then he is alive.

PR. Nay, he is dead and slain by Edward's hands.

PA. In thy foul throat thou liest! Queen Margaret saw thy

murderous sword smoking in his blood. (*Points to the body of HENRY VI.*) Didst thou not kill *this* king?

PR. I grant ye.

PA. Dost grant me, hedgehog? Then God grant me too thou mayest be damned for that wicked deed! O, he was gentle, mild and virtuous!

PR. The better for the King of Heaven that hath him.

PA. He *is* in heaven, where thou shalt never come. Thou art unfit for any place but hell.

PR. Yes, one place else, if you will hear me name it.

PA. Some dungeon.

PR. Your bedchamber.

PA. Ill rest betide the chamber where thou liest!

PR. Gentle Lady Anne, is not the causer of the timeless deaths of those Plantagenets, Henry and Edward, as blameful as the executioner?

PA. *Thou* was the cause and most accursed effect.

PR. *Your* beauty was the *cause* of that effect - your beauty, that did haunt me in my sleep to undertake the death of all the world.

PA. If I thought that, I tell thee these nails should rent that beauty from my cheeks. (*Bares her claws.*)

PR (*grabbing her wrists*). These eyes could not endure that beauty's wreck. It is a quarrel most unnatural, to be ravenged on him that loveth thee.

PA (*pulling herself away from him*). It is a quarrel just and reasonable, to be revenged on him that killed my husband.

PR. He that bereft thee, lady, of thy husband, did it to help thee to a *better* husband.

PA. Name him.

PR. Plantagenet.

PA. Why, that was he.

PR. The selfsame name, but one of better nature.

PA. Where is he?

PR (*pointing to himself*). Here. (*She spits at him.*) Why dost thou spit at me?

PA. Would it were mortal poison, for thy sake!

PR. Never came poison from so sweet a place.

PA. Never hung poison on a fouler toad. Out of my sight! Thou dost infect mine eyes.

PR. Thine yes, sweet lady, have infected mine, for now they kill me with a living death. (*She looks scornfully at him.*) Teach not thy lip such scorn, for it was made for kissing, lady, not for such contempt. If thy revengeful heart cannot forgive, lo, here I lend thee this sharp-pointed sword, which if thou please to hide in this true breast, and let the soul forth that adoreth thee. I lay it naked to the deadly stroke, and humbly beg the death upon my knee. (*He gives her his dagger, then kneels before her and opens his shirt. She makes a move as if to strike, but pauses.*) Nay, do not pause: for *I did* kill King Henry - but 'twas thy beauty that provoked me. (*She drops the dagger and turns away from him.*) Take up the sword again, or take me up.

PA. Arise, dissembler: though I wish thy death, I will not be thy executioner. (*He stands.*)

PR. Say, then, my peace is made.

PA. That shalt thou know hereafter.

PR. But shall I live in hope?

PA. All men, I hope, live so.

PR (*takes a ring from his finger*). Vouchsafe to wear this ring.

PA. To take is not to give. (*He takes her hand and puts the ring on her finger.*)

PR. Look how my ring encompasseth thy finger, even so thy breast encloseth my poor heart. Wear both of them, for both of them are thine. Bid me farewell.

PA. 'Tis more than you deserve; but since you teach me how to flatter you, imagine I have said farewell already. (*She returns to the Gallery followed by the two BEARERS and the BODY. They take their seats.*)

PR. Was ever a woman in this humor wooed? Was ever a woman in this humor won? I'll have her. Shine out, fair sun, till I have bought a glass that I may see my shadow as I pass. (*He returns to his seat.*)

CHARITY (*coming center*). I ask again, my lady: you say none of this was true?

ANNE. None of it. I gave my heart to Richard when we

were both still children together in the gardens of Middleham. I gave him my hand willingly when he freed me from Clarence's tyranny.

CHARITY. Clarence's tyranny? Please explain to the court.

ANNE. My father gave my older sister, Isabelle, to Richard's brother, the Duke of Clarence, in marriage. When my father died, Clarence came into control of my father's vast estates except for my portion. At that time, I was engaged to Edward of Lancaster. When Edward was killed at Tewkesbury, Clarence, now as head of my family, took over my estates as well. He refused to let Richard even see me. Clarence wanted everything for himself. He wasn't interested in my welfare at all, just my lands. He ... he forced me to go into hiding, disguised as a cook's maid in a...a public house.

CHARITY. Surely a deep humiliation for so noble a lady. What happened then?

ANNE. Richard searched for me, found me and rescued me from Clarence's control. We were then married, to my everlasting joy.

CHARITY. One final question, my lady. Did your husband ever try to kill you?

ANNE. No, never! He was the one true love of my life. He defied *both* his brothers, yes, even the King, to marry me and ours was the happiest marriage of them all.

CHARITY. Thank you, my lady. I have no further questions. (*She returns to her seat.*)

TIME. Cross-examination?

CHARITY. We ask our honored colleague to keep his questioning of this witness brief as her health is somewhat delicate.

HISTORY (*rising*). Thank you, I shall endeavor to do so. Lady Anne, if you loved Richard so much from your childhood, why did you marry Edward of Lancaster?

ANNE. I wasn't *married* to Edward. We were merely engaged. As a fourteen-year-old girl, I had no choice but to obey my father's wishes. The Earl of Warwick was called "The Kingmaker" for good reason. His army could make or break either side in the Wars of the Roses. He married his daughters to heirs of the Yorks and Lancasters, so that no matter which side eventually won, he would be father-in-law to a king. It was purely a political arrangement. Love had nothing to do with it.

HISTORY. And did you learn to love Prince Edward?

ANNE. I barely knew him. He was always away somewhere, fighting, during our brief betrothal.

HISTORY. Do you feel you know your husband Richard's character?

ANNE. Oh, yes!

HISTORY. And do you feel in your heart that he could not have killed *anyone*?

ANNE (*uncomfortable*). I didn't say that. Of course, I knew he had killed men. He was a soldier. But he was not the evil, cold-blooded murderer that you accuse him of being.

HISTORY. And you don't believe he had his own nephews murdered to get the throne for himself?

ANNE. No! He loved children. He was always kind to them. We had a son, Edward, whom we loved dearly. Both of us were deeply saddened when he died a year after Richard was crowned. We also reared several other children in our household - children whose fathers had been killed in battle. If he did this, how could he turn around and kill his own flesh and blood whom he was honor-bound to protect! Do you think for one minute that I would allow myself to be crowned Queen if the price of that crown had been my nephews' blood? No! Never! I'll not believe it! (*She bursts into tears. RICHARD comes to her side.*)

RICHARD. Your Honor, the strain of this trial has been too much for my wife. I beg she be excused.

TIME. Counselor?

HISTORY. I have no further questions.

TIME. The witness may stand down. (*ANNE leaves the witness chair and is escorted back to her seat by RICHARD.*)

CHARITY. Your Honor, the defense rests.

TIME. Then, counselors, present your summations for the jury. Prosecution first.

(QUEEN and the COUNTESS re-enter and sit.)

RUMOR *(rising and coming center stage)*. Your Honor and ladies and gentlemen of the jury, despite a brave show of emotional upheaval and outright denials, the facts of our case against Richard III stand. While we concede that he was not the deformed monster of Shakespearean fame, nevertheless the prosecution maintains that his crimes of murder and treason against the crown are irrefutable. By his own admission, Richard III has killed men in his time - men, not a man, but several. Who knows how many? Killing is like anything else. Once you can do it for the first time, it gets easier after that. The defendant claims that he had no hand in the deaths of his own brother, the Duke of Clarence, nor against Henry VI, rightful King of England - yet was he not Constable of England at the time? One of the duties of this office is to carry out or have carried out any royal warrants of execution. Can we truly believe that, just because he was out of town, he didn't know anything about Clarence's death? A most unusual death, if you recall - drowning in a barrel of malmesy wine. Does that sound like the choice of a condemned man or that of his executioners? Or, rather, does that sound more like the cruel and final practical joke of a vengeful little brother? And the two Little Princes in the Tower - consider them. They were supposed to be in Richard's safekeeping. He kept them safe all right - so safe that no one ever heard from them again. So safe, that even their bodies disappeared from sight for almost 150 years, when the bones of two young boys, aged approximately nine and twelve, were discovered buried under a stair exactly where Sir Thomas More said they would be all those years before. And how did Sir Thomas know? From the recorded confession of James

Tyrrel. And how did Tyrrel know? By his own admission, he *put* them there! But the defendant, Richard III, claims to have no knowledge of the Princes' whereabouts - alive or dead. All he can say is: "I didn't do it!" In the space of two short years, the reign of Richard III was one of fear, terror and murder. Thank heavens he was the last Plantagenet! England couldn't have survived too many more Lord Protectors such as *he*! Henry Tudor, Earl of Richmond and later Henry VII, did us all a favor when he defeated Richard on Bosworth Field on August 22, 1485. Ladies and gentlemen of the jury, you can do no more than your duty to bring in a verdict *against* Richard III. He is guilty of the blackest sins of mankind. He richly deserves his infamous reputation. Vote against this blackened monster! I thank you. (*She returns to her seat and sits.*)

TIME. The defense will now speak. (*RICHARD rises and comes center.*)

RICHARD. Ladies and gentlemen of the jury, I stand here before you as I have always stood, alone and in my own defense. My reign, as the prosecution pointed out, was but two years - one of the shortest in English history and yet it is *I* who am called the most evil king in that history - not Henry VIII, nor King John, nor even Oliver Cromwell, but, I, Richard III, and why? Because in that final battle on Bosworth Field, I lost my kingdom, my crown, my life and my reputation to a far-flung, illegitimate claimant to the throne, Henry Tudor. History is always written by the winners. It was my greatest misfortune that *my* history - the one which would give tribute to Tudor and show *him* to be England's savior - *that* history was written by one of the greatest saints of the Catholic Church and by the greatest literary figure in the world. I refer, of course, to Saint Thomas More and to William Shakespeare. Did either man mean to write my story as *real* history despite the titles of their works? No, these Tudor-inspired authors did not. Sir Thomas, by his own admission, wrote an incomplete rough draft of a manuscript which was not published until *after* his own execution. Shakespeare, by *his* admission, wrote a play to please a Tudor queen and to entertain the people. Did either of these so-called historians tell of the good works which I accomplished during my short time on the throne? Did they tell you of the college I founded in York, or the trade agreements I established with Europe? Did they mention the improvements I made in the judicial system especially for the poor, such as a trial by jury of peers, the establishment of reasonable bail or the translation of the law from Latin into common English? Did they write that I instituted financial reforms after thirty years of civil war, or that I built several churches in God's honor or that I encouraged book printing and the establishment of libraries? Of course not, for all these works would make Richard III look too good and reflect badly on the upstart Tudor who killed him. But no matter how evil the histories of More and Shakespeare paint me, both writers could not escape mentioning my courage. I was the last English king to die in the line of battle. I did not hide behind my knights as Henry Tudor did. I was fighting to protect my kingdom from invasion. (*The PLAYERS have risen and are quietly moving toward the center as RICHARD, remembering the battle, moves to the right.*) Though Shakespeare gave me chilling nightmares in the final act, he could not help but write for me a stirring final speech: "Go, gentlemen, every man to his charge. Conscience is but a word that cowards use. Our strong arms be our conscience, swords our law!" (*PR's voice joins RICHARD's as PR moves to center stage.*)

PR and RICHARD. March on! Join bravely! Let us to it pell-mell, if not to heaven, then hand in hand to hell ... (*RICHARD breaks off as PR continues the speech on his own.*)

PR. Let's whip these stragglers over the seas again. If we be conquered, let *men* conquer us, and not these bastard Britains. Shall these enjoy our lands? Hark! I hear their drum. Fight, gentlemen of England! Fight, bold yeomen! Draw, archers, draw your arrows to the head! Spur your proud horses hard, and ride in blood! Amaze the heavens with your broken staves! (*Enter a MESSENGER.*) What says Lord Stanley? Will he bring his power?

MESSENGER. My lord, he doth deny to come.

(*Enter CATESBY.*)

CATESBY. My lord, the enemy is past the marsh.

PR. A thousand hearts are great within my bosom! Advance our standards, set upon our foes. Our ancient word of courage, fair St. George, inspire us with the spleen of fiery dragons! Upon them! Victory sits on our helms! (*Freezes as CATESBY moves forward.*)

CATESBY (*to the audience*). The King enacts more wonders than a man, daring an opposite to every danger: his horse is slain, and all on foot he fights, seeking for Richmond, the Tudor, in the throat of death. (*PR comes to life with drawn sword.*)

PR. A horse! A horse! My kingdom for a horse!

CATESBY. Withdraw, my lord. I'll help you to a horse.

PR. Shame! I have set my life upon a cast and I will stand the hazard of the dice. I think there be six Richmonds in the field; five have I slain today instead of him. A horse! A horse!

(*PR is surrounded by the PLAYERS who pull him down out of sight of the audience. They mime stabbing him, then step back as RICHMOND appears from the back. PR lies dead. One of the PLAYERS lifts his crown off his head and hands it to RICHMOND who puts it on. RICHMOND comes down to front.*)

RICHMOND. God and your arms be praised, victorious friends! The day is ours; the bloody dog is dead. Inter the men of name as became their births. Proclaim a pardon to the soldiers who fled that in submission will return to us. We will unite the White Rose and the Red. Smile heaven upon this fair conjunction. Now civil wounds are stopped, peace lives again: that she may long live here, God say amen! (*PLAYERS with PR's body quietly return to their seats. RICHARD, who has been in a trance, slowly comes out of it.*)

RICHARD. But the noble Tudor did not honor *my* body, my mangled and bleeding body, the work of his henchmen. He had me stripped, put a criminal's collar around my neck and threw me over the rump of a pack horse. As the horse was led across the bridge away from the battlefield, my head struck each post rail in turn - my head, once anointed and crowned. The Tudor paid ten pounds, one shilling for my wooden coffin and he complained that this small sum was too much. I was buried without honor or mourners in the Grey Friars churchyard, but I did not rest in peace. The Tudor did not permit it. Later, my coffin was dug up and used as a water trough for horses. My bones were thrown into the River Soar. The Tudors and Yorks and Lancasters rest side by side today in Windsor and Westminster under great marble monuments. My bones lie deep in the river's mud, unknown and unmourned. Thus ended Richard III.

Did I kill men? Yes, I won't deny it but only in battle or for treason. "Loyalty Binds Me" was my motto and I was loyal to the death for England. In return, what loyalty has been shown me? Ask those bones in the riverbank. Ask the hundred thousand playgoers who have seen Shakespeare's *Richard III*. Ask any schoolboy in the street and watch him spit on my name. Do I deserve this? Am I worse than any other ruler who ever sat upon England's throne? Ladies and gentlemen of the jury, *now* is the moment for which I have waited so long. Now *you* can erase the slanders of five centuries. If you believe me to be a better man than History has portrayed me, then vote *for* my good name. My fate is in your hands. You have the power to right the wrongs that have been done to me. I beg for justice. I beg for truth. I am in your power. Thank you. (*He returns to his seat.*)

TIME (*to the audience*). Ladies and gentlemen of the jury, you have heard the testimony and weighed the evidence for and against the name of Richard III. If you feel that this man has been given undue slander against him by History down through the ages, then vote "Yes." If you feel that Richard III did, in fact, cold-bloodedly commit the crimes of which he is accused and thereby warrants the reputation as the most evil king of England, then you must vote "No." We will now call for a vocal vote. Mr. Bailiff.

BAILIFF (*coming to the edge of the stage*). All who vote *for* Richard III please signify by voting "Aye." (*Pause while the audience responds.*) All who vote *against* Richard III please signify by voting "Nay." (*Pause while the audience responds.*) Your Honor, the verdict in the case of Richard III is . . . .

THE DOUBLE ENDING

IF THE JURY VOTES RICHARD III AS "GUILTY":

TIME. Richard III, rise. (*RICHARD and CHARITY stand and face TIME.*) Richard III, you have been duly tried under the law and have been judged guilty as charged. Therefore, I sentence you to live out Eternity in everlasting shame and perdition. Your name shall evermore by synonymous with Evil; your reputation shall henceforth be blackened and all men shall turn against you. You shall have no hope of redemption; no hope of pardon for your crimes against humanity. May your soul burn in the everlasting bonfires of Hell. Go, and shun forevermore this company. (*Strikes the gavel once and rises.*) This trial is declared over. (*All freeze. Curtain/blackout.*)

IF THE JURY VOTES RICHARD III "NOT GUILTY":

TIME. Richard III, arise. (*RICHARD and CHARITY rise*

and face the judge.) You have been duly tried under the law and have been judged not guilty of the charges against your reputation. Therefore, you are free to go forth among this company. Furthermore, I charge all here present in this court and jury to henceforth and forevermore to uphold the good name and reputation of this most injured of kings, Richard III. *(Strikes the gavel once and rises.)* Case dismissed. *(All freeze. Curtain/blackout.)*

PRODUCTION NOTES

"THE FINAL TRIAL OF RICHARD III" is a one-set courtroom drama taking place in Eternity which lends itself to simple stage design or for use in the classroom. The Gallery or Spectator section is set on a diagonal running from upstage left down to almost mid-stage with a center aisle. Directly in front of the Gallery are two small tables or desks with two chairs each. The upstage desk is for the prosecution and the downstage is the defense. Upstage center is the CLERK's table and chair, facing forward. The raised judge's bench is downstage right with the witness box to the right of the bench and closest to the audience/jury. The center stage section is left open and clear to allow for the play-within-the-play. The stretcher for the body of HENRY VI is open and pre-set behind the Gallery at the farthest point upstage left. It will be out of sight of the audience when the actors are seated. A curtain is not necessary but a nice touch.

The lighting is general with possible area lighting on the open center stage area for the Shakespearean scenes.

Costumes are simple. TIME should appear in judicial robes. As the trial format is American rather than British, HISTORY, RUMOR and the CLERK can be dressed as they would appear in a modern American court. The BAILIFF is dressed either in a suit or policeman's uniform. CHARITY can either be in modern day business clothes or in a more stylized costume representing her Virtue. The historical characters: RICHARD, ANNE, ELIZABETH, MORE, SHAKESPEARE and THE COUNTESS OF DESMOND, can be in the clothing of their period, or again, in stylized versions, or even modern dress, at the director's discretion. The PLAYERS should be in loose-fitting rehearsal clothing - tights and tunics if they are appearing as the Lord Chamberlain's Men or in modern day clothing if they decide to appear as members of the Lord Chamberlain's Men. (*"Old actors never die; they just play away."*)

Props are simple. The majority belong to the PLAYERS who carry them on in a small prop bag. (*See separate list for props.*)

The play's running time is approximately one and a half hours and should be presented without interruption or intermission in order to allow the case to build up in dramatic intensity and to keep the jury (*audience*) from comparing notes during the trial. There are 24 parts in all; 8 women and 16 men, although some of the PLAYERS can be women playing men's parts. HISTORY and the CLERK can be either male or female.

A SHORT NOTE ON THE CHARACTERIZATION OF RICHARD III

"THE FINAL TRIAL OF RICHARD III" is written so that the character of Richard III can be interpreted in one of two ways: as very sympathetic and innocent or as an evil man trying to cover up his crimes and dodge accusations. Depending upon which characterization the director chooses, the jury will vote accordingly, in most cases.

If RICHARD is innocent and wishes to appear sympathetic, all his lines should be delivered with openness and directness. His concern for his wife is a true indication of his love for her. His final speech is a plea for justice.

On the other hand, if the director wishes to portray RICHARD guilty as charged, (*except for the physical deformity*) then the lines should be delivered with cynicism and double meanings. Direct accusations are hotly denied. An attempted cover-up should be obvious, especially in RICHARD's explanation of the disappearance of the Little Princes. Notice that RICHARD's final speech does not once refute any of the charges, but instead he begs for the jury's sympathy.

Of the two characterizations, the guilty one is the harder to maintain, but it is infinitely more interesting.

PROP LIST

TIME: a gavel.

HISTORY: Exhibit A: copy of More's *History of Richard III*.

RICHARD III - HISTORY: Exhibit B: copy (*modern playbook*) of Shakespeare's *Richard III*.

CHARITY: Exhibit C: copy of the indictment against the Duke of Clarence.

PLAYER RICHARD: a simple crown, two rings, a warrant, a dagger, a sword.

MURDERERS: daggers.

HENRY TUDOR: sword.

HENRY VI: stretcher and cover.

BRACKENBURY: key ring.

CLERK: steno book and quill pen.